Andy Allan

Within the Slide of Wind

Indigo Dreams Publishing

First Edition: Within the Slide of Wind
First published in Great Britain in 2018 by:
Indigo Dreams Publishing
24, Forest Houses
Cookworthy Moor
Halwill
Beaworthy
Devon
EX21 5UU

www.indigodreams.co.uk

Andy Allan has asserted his right under the Copyright, Designs and Patents Act 1988 to be identified as the author of this work. ©2018 Andy Allan

ISBN 978-1-910834-95-4

British Library Cataloguing in Publication Data. A CIP record for this book can be obtained from the British Library.

Designed and typeset in Palatino Linotype by Indigo Dreams.
Cover design Ronnie Goodyer at Indigo Dreams
Printed and bound in Great Britain by 4edge Ltd.

Papers used by Indigo Dreams are recyclable products made from wood grown in sustainable forests following the guidance of the Forest Stewardship Council.

For Morag

Acknowledgements

An extra-special thank you goes to my award-winning publishers at Indigo Dreams, Ronnie Goodyer and Dawn Bauling. Special thanks also to Eileen Carney Hulme, Glynis Stainton and Carol Argyris for their friendly support, sage advice and constructive criticism.

Versions of many of the poems in this collection have appeared in poetry magazines, in journals, in anthologies, on internet sites as well as being prize-winning entries in competitions, so grateful thanks to the editors of Raum, Poetry Cornwall, Reach Poetry, Northwords Now, Poetry Scotland, Sarasvati, The Dawntreader, The Stanza Poetry Map of Scotland, Words in the Landscape – Anthology, Soundwaves – Anthology, the Callander Haiku – Anthology, Bold Type – Anthology.

Thanks also to the Nairn Bookshop and the Olive Tree Café at Logie, who have a framed copies of *Turning Leaves* and *Monday Morning*, on wall-display; to Sally Evans for encouragement over the years at the wonderful Callander Poetry Festival and of course to my writerly friends in Forres and in places further afield.

Also by Andy Allan:

Breath of Dragons, IDP, 2015.

CONTENTS

Within the Slide of Wind

A room with no books is like a body with no soul –
Cicero

Shadows of Belonging

Dark skerries glisten on the world's edge,
delight surging through white spume.
Overhead, a gull soars with your endless laughter,
sailing with me through long, blue yesterdays.
In rising winds and ocean agitation,
huge breakers pound on silver sands where
shifting shingle rattles in a churning rush,
retreating hush . . . before they crash once more.

In dunes, where gale-tugged grasses flail,
my mind drifts under scudding clouds,
shifts through lonely shafts of sunlight.
Memories gather, hovering at my shoulder
as I taste again your sea-salt-breath.
On a stiffening breeze I see your dissolving
footprints scrawled on wind-whipped sand.

Clouds race with wind-shadows,
biting sand-storms scour the empty beach,
unable to erase our shared past.
We will always belong in this place
immersed in its isolation,
rooted to this rugged shore.

Summer Evening, Eriskay

Inspired by two paintings: 'Washday, Eriskay' and 'Cockle Strand, Barra,'
by Alex Summers.

A white speck screams, soars high over flailing machair.
The cottage squats in an ocean of writhing turbulence,
yellows fading to grey, a world of streaming grasses,
of blues and greens, of sea and sky, of sand and wind,
restless turquoise waters darkening through moments.

Beyond the dry-stone wall a singing rope
strains between wind-blasted posts, their silvered
shoulders leaning into the ceaseless blast.
Three new white pillow-cases thrash the island air,
struggling for freedom, desperate for flight.

A restless sea, reddens in the west. Breakers rumble,
their glistening flood pouring over dark rocks.
White clouds, scudding on wet-sand's mirror,
fade in the growing gloom, the orange tin-roof,
undimmed, a beacon, gathering stars.

On Culbin's Lonely Coast

Cold-air brushes tree-clad dunes,
soughs through pine-boughs.
Dark trees stretch bony fingers
to North's thin light,
fumble through the ceaseless,
sifting, wave-sounds of the firth.
The staccato rattle of woodpecker
heralds momentary silence.
An oyster-catcher's 'peeps' merge
into a fresh cacophony of birdsong.

The lonely lagoon's grey skin
trembles in sea-air's bluster, but,
close to shore it's still and silvered,
a silent mirror where clouds sail.
I'm lost, absorbed, in a world where
noisy sandpipers dart and call,
ululate into tenuous tranquillity.
A disgruntled heron, shoulders hunched,
shrugs and almost sighs, moves on with
tired resolve, each precise movement,
a dance-step in his grey display.

I fill my lungs with cold, clean air
and lose all sense of time,
immersed in woodland audio-mumble.
Gathering shower-clouds shroud the firth,
and all-too-soon, the rain arrives,
large drops, splatter-pattering.
The woodland stills as I rise to leave,
my hushed smile drifting on the wind.

Just After Dawn

Gathering light-needles
grow into bright fingers,
their low-glow brushing
the eastern cheeks of trees,
green-leaves tinted gold.
Shredded sheets of morning drift,
scattered vapour veils low hills
indistinct in distance.
In increasing brightness,
remnants of fleeting dreams
dwindle to transient shadows.
Ascending sun gains strength,
fresh breath ruffles the
land's green surface,
bathing it in growing birdsong.

Dava Moor

Squatting in cloud-shadow and sunbeams,
a sturdy hut of dark railway-sleepers
emerges from the veil of distance.
On embankment's long green curve,
a light-speckled carpet of short grasses
and wind-twinkling wildflowers
light the way to this linesman's haven.

Yellowed swaying grasses swish
the windy silence, play through
strands of twisted, rusting wire.
Defiant weathered posts persist,
resist the years, resist the power
that's scoured their pale grey skin;
grey-green lichen beards
fluttering in cool summer air.

Dark silhouette of skylark bounces
on blustery undulating air,
rising, falling in an empty heaven,
song soaring with the wind.
Passing the lonely ruin at Auchlochan,
the old railway line rests, content,
settled in this slumbering glen.

Rushing air sweeps the treeless slopes,
whipping waves of heather surge
beneath boisterous cloud-shadows,
stifling glare, softening light.
Ancient gods dwell here, filtering
eternal winds, whistling, resisting time.
Bowing to the touch of air's caress,
the lonely moor listens,
whispers its time-worn secrets.

Sleepers

Poised on embankment's edge,
megaliths of ancient timber
stab a relentless sky.
Stark, dark, weathered, worn,
silhouettes of ominous fingers,
stretching, reaching for yesterday.
Icy air slips through gaps,
filters through splits and spaces,
sinuous currents sifting,
drifting beyond time.
Lost and lonely sentinels,
they linger still,
warding this deserted line
on desolate Dava moor.

Season Turning

Light is soft as time's tide turns.
A fat pigeon swoops through
sparse, yellow leaf-fall.
Birch-confetti lemon-twirls,
twists and glitters through
low sun's gentle glimmer.
Overhead, skeins of geese
voice incessant songs of leaving,
their wing-beat-rhythm,
tight as galley slaves.

Feisty blue-tits flit and dance
on sheds, poke at wooden fences,
hanging, dangling, insect picking,
searching in dark corners,
oblivious of what's to come.
In the trees and overhead
the air is full of agitated crows,
unsettled by their knowledge,
circling, cawing their warning.

Restless boughs scrape the silence,
tremble beneath gathering grey.
An urgent blackbird calls,
darkening skies grow heavy,
light fades in the West.
Arriving almost unnoticed,
Winter slides in on light winds,
slips into fields and woodlands
trailing soft white kisses.

A Woodland Encounter

Beneath heavy, lichen-covered limbs,
wiry jaundiced grasses shiver
in Autumn's fading breath.
Orange needles mottle mossy blankets
that shroud the forest's wooden toes.
Storm debris litters the woodland floor,
branches, twigs and long-dead
tree-trunks rot on roe-deer runs.
On thin pale skies, silhouettes of
chaffinches shoal into swaying,
bouncing boughs of larch.
Low, angled shafts of sunlight
pierce birch thickets, redden pines
and stripe the silent forest track.

In gentle air-ripples, agitated leaves
rasp their sibilant song, its murmur
sliding through flickering spaces.
Without warning, grit grates underfoot.
A sable head shoots up. Alert, alarmed,
dark wide eyes blink innocence,
surprise, lithe body poised for flight,
frozen by uncertainty. Moments tick.
Whispers drift. An ear flicks.
A flapping pigeon snaps attention's
fragile grip and the doe is gone.
I exhale slowly, hesitant breath-
clouds condensing in cold air
and a legacy of enigmatic silence.

Blades of Death

Air-drifting in death,
lifeless in failing light,
a golden tide is tumbling.
Autumn bounty, saw-toothed,
fluttering through space,
shaped like ancient Celtic blades.
Clustered together, leaves lie
motionless in cold damp air,
soft, spongy, wet underneath,
on top, wrinkled like old skin.
In weak sunlight, a velvet,
caramel comfort of moist,
soft, toffee-brown,
drying into crisp, rough drifts,
rustling the forest world
into winter's sleep.

Life is Deep

Brown-tinged, peaty water tumbles,
a restless flow roaring into dingy
depths below the cascade's rush.
A brass reel ticks, line slips
through numb and frozen fingers.
Rising through flickering silver,
the ragged bait hangs, dripping.
Another wriggling sacrifice is chosen,
cast into the icy unknown,
where bubbles float and
white foam gathers.

Air-blasted, gnarled and devious,
the old rowan sings in the wind.
The shimmering surface of a dark
pool sheltering in her mythic shadow,
reveals nothing of the ancient resident
lurking in the gloom.
Indifferent, he ignores the line, watches
his impetuous descendants, bite.
Unmoved, uncaring, he flicks a fin.
He's seen it all before.

Within the Slide of Wind

Birches lift and swell in swirling
flutters as the trees sing,
their voices like wave-dragged shingle,
shush, shush, in the constant rush of air.
A grey-white blanket hides the sun,
obscures the high blue heavens,
as I walk this slick and empty road,
in the aftermath of rain.

Soft light flickers on drops of liquid
silver, flashing, dripping, dangling,
glittering like jewels.
Air slips through bouncing boughs to
set rustling yellow leaves a-dancing.
Chittering chaffinches chase through
fragmented thought, cavort in shoals,
dart into tossing tree-shadow.

Like magic they reappear, slipping
through bowed wires, swooping
over grim grey buildings,
skating on glossy slate.
Breathing deep my spirits soar,
invigorated on this wild dreich day,
this glorious singing cold wet land,
this place where I belong.

The Wren

Whispering wind-murmur masks
each inadvertent sound she makes
as she watches from dim thickets,
concealed from roving, probing eyes.
Tic-tic-tic, she scolds, flickering
briefly into sight, bobbing, posing,
calling once more, before
darting back to darkness.
Tiny sister of wraiths and shadows,
sweetheart of hedgerows and shrubberies;
a secret witness, informer of owls.
She calls again, *Tic-tic-tic*.
Unseen, hidden, her sisters respond,
their tic-a-tic chorus echoing through
sunbeams and hazy silence.
Watchers in the woods,
sisters of shadow.

Autumn in Assynt

High above the white-toothed loch,
ripples in time caress sombre hills.
Signals of change weave
across speckled wooded slopes.
A dark stag stands alone,
defiant on a bright horizon,
stark emblem of harsh renewal.

Green vibrance fades with
each shortening day,
tired birches huddle in hollows,
their ragged canopy growing
dull as hillside bracken,
yellowing, turning sickly, pale,
a landscape haunted by ghosts of colour.

Atlantic gales stalk Assynt's coast,
blustery ice-breaths shiver
through frail branches.
Squally showers
beat weeping thickets,
pale leaves death-twirling
through damp yesterdays.

Relics to stubborn survival,
trees endure through death,
white boles like marble monuments.
Antlers clash amidst alders,
outrage roared at growing mortality,
defiant challenge bellowed to
approaching winter, to the world.

High Above the Black Loch's Skin

Beyond the rocky shore below,
beneath ragged veils of rain,
jagged, wind-driven, patterns race
upon the black loch's skin.
The ground is sodden, spongy,
feet scrabble over cold, bare rock,
tramp through thin heather and
plouter the skirts of ice-pools.

Bathed in soft, winter light,
Chuinneag's looming presence
dominates the southern sky.
Lashing winds tear at a scene
washed of colour where
stunted birches cling,
high in rock cracks, above
the reach of hungry deer.
Scanning the moor, I trace
the route of an old pack trail,
it's hidden presence revealed by
low sun's light and shadow.

Rootless melodies of leaf-song
whistle through absent branches
that tremble only in memory.
Assynt weeps for its lost trees.
Their story surrounds me,
scribbled in light flickers,
air-breaths mumbling memories
of closeness with this land.

The mountain, 'Chuinneag,' Scots Gaelic, meaning a milking pail,
'Quinag,' in English.

Dreaming by the Broken Gate

Primitive emblem of strength and power,
warm in his tangled ginger coat,
he stands alone, defying winter.
Long horns gouge the clear blue sky,
piercing dark eyes stare
through a yellowed fringe.
Dilating nostrils, wet and pink,
send breath-cloud-geysers snorting
into morning's patience.

His field of short grey grass is frosted,
white-edged with rime and silence.
An illusion of containment,
the dilapidated wooden gate,
leans towards terminal collapse,
one end hanging on a loop
of rusting fence-wire.

Impassive, motionless in frozen,
hoof-churned mud,
he dreams of another place,
of lingering in tree-shadow
where soft morning-mist
brushes lush green meadows.

Blank Canvas

Footfalls crunch the frosty silence,
ice-winds shiver through a moonlit
backdrop, every sound deadened.
Dark trees loom, ghosts poised,
their transient shadows scribbling
on pristine fields of white.
Lying on my back, in snow, I feel
so small beneath this huge, wide sky,
this empty space hanging high
above our planet's face.
Staring in wonder like a child,
I scan a gossamer darkness
restless with tremulous stars.
Adrift, I float through endless time
sifting possibilities, seeding
measureless dreams.

Loch an Eilein

The Cairngorms loom
on a spark-speckled skyscape.
A floating causeway sweeps south,
a path of ivory-silk shimmering
on dark choppy waters.
Straight from the great luminous
pearl of the rising moon, it slips,
two-thirds already breasting
the shoulder of Creag Dubh.
A lapping suck and gentle slap the
only sounds on that dim loch-shore.

Gloom gathers, hills and stars fade,
backlight snuffed by descending grey.
Soft flakes drift on the rising whisper
of icy air's caress.
A heavy sky grows close and low,
as a million snowflakes tumble
through the hush of darkness, a
silent white suicide in cold black water.

Cold Winter Beach

The rush of waves sounds strange
in calm illusion's hush,
the sigh of each retreat, a pause,
the soft sift as shingle shifts,
shadow footprint smudges
fore-toiled in heavy sand.

Discarded secrets strewn in sunlight,
hint-dropping, message-mumbling
through empty silence.
A label-less plastic bottle lies half-buried,
questions posed by cloudy contents,
the shredded cord tied round its neck.

Snagged thought, eye-caught by a tiny
flutter, old-tale memories woken,
a white banner? A fairy marker?
A pale-feather caught in the deep-red
morass of drying bladder-wrack,
discarded storm debris.

Beyond the marram dunes,
deep in whispers,
frail golden trees crouch in low light,
the hidden sun flickering,
trembling through bough-sway
on this dying afternoon.

Songs of Loss and Hope

Relentless gales roar over water,
long white scars rake on restless black.
Dying Winter rasps my face,
dunes cower beneath slate-blue skies.
I sit, high in wind-whipped grasses,
patrolling gulls struggle in turbulent air.

Sleek seals lie in undulating clusters,
scattered like thrown satin cushions
over cold, wet sand.
Wailing voices mewl lingering laments,
endless songs of death and loss.
Beach companions, dancing dunlin
and busy oystercatchers, ignore their cries.

Black, massive, menacing, he bursts
from dark water roaring his challenge,
crashing onto the crowded beach,
bellowing his belligerence.
Shuffling cows and rivals scatter.
Inured to pain, his people survive
singing of stubborn endurance.

As if from nowhere, five white swans,
untainted, pure, fly low over darkness,
their passage silent in the rising wind.
Vigorous, vital, sleek and strong,
unmoved by plaintive songs and cries.
Precursory messengers of light,
Spring's first arrows of hope,
they cross the bay, surge upriver.

Highland School

Shouts and giggles soak
into shadowy moorland,
sing through naked branches,
sigh through bowed wires.
Innocence, at ease
in icy winds and isolation,
dancing defiance under
low and darkening skies.

Standing alone, basking
in the joy of generations,
the building radiates influence;
a haven of belonging,
an anchor in turbulence,
a beacon in the dark.
The solid wooden door,
an open gateway to the world.

The Noisy Silence

In shimmering heat, voice-murmurs
thrum through open windows,
a distant engine's grumble grows,
rubber rumbles on warm tarmac.
Wandering bees drone through mazes
of bright-blossom and birdsong.
Breathing deep, Old Willow's
streaming canopy inflates, deflates,
in swells of sultry, summer, air.
Wafted high, tiny spiders weave
daydreams in dazzle, sailing silken
threads glinting in bright light.

Glossy leaves tremble, send sparks
flashing where swallows dart and dive,
dark bodies streak in sunlight's dazzle,
delight scrawled on cloudless blue.
A white, nectar-drunk, butterfly's
raggedy flight-path winds round greenery.
Sparrows flit through flickering foliage,
burbling pigeons hide in tree-shade,
echoes cooing through clouds of haze
where bustling insects buzz.
Cat-wary, dark eyes sparkling,
a watchful blackbird basks,
wings spread on roof-tiles,
poised to still this noisy silence.

On Such a Day

I breathe deep, my smile beaming
through cold-wind's breath.
Silent skitters of ragged white
race on clear, bright blue,
dissolving as they pass.
Expectations soar, breathless
joy muffled in plunging air.

Trees heave and moan,
their silhouettes flouncing on
waves of rampaging grasses,
their bough-shadows bouncing
on pale sunlit fields.
Air slips through flailing branches,
demanding that they dance,
singing, whistling to the throb
and rhythm of humming wires.

Lines of washing claw the sky,
slapping, cracking their exuberance.
I feel I want to run and shout as
brittle leaves scour the stony path
rattling, rustling, rushing nowhere,
doing everything that matters
on such a day.

Seaforth Villa, Carron, 1954

Under leaf-sway, my sister
lay asleep in the big grey pram.
Granny smiled at me, put down her tea,
patted her lap and held out her arms.
Come here, sit on my knee, she said.
We looked at the cover of the book.
It's Rupert, she whispered as
if sharing an important secret.

Our heads touched and I breathed the
soapy-wool scent of her cardigan.
Reading, she paused often to explain.
After a while she closed the book,
smiled and lowered me to the ground.
Was that nice? Did you like it?
Looking up at her, I nodded,
saw puffy clouds, the same colour
as her hair, drifting on summer's blue.

Drawn to the upturned wooden
wheelbarrow, I climbed on top,
whirled the wheel and made it roar.
A sudden shrill whistle sounded,
the chittering birds fell silent.
That's 'The Puggie,' she said,
you know, the train from Aberlour.
I can't remember a time when
Granny wasn't smiling.

Change of Mind

I checked the living-room
in seconds, found nothing.
Their round faces closed in on me,
my blurted question drew grins,
I think I was holding my breath.
Is it a Winchester rifle?
Eyes-twinkled at my uncertainty.
Happy birthday, they chirped,
drowning me in laughter,
then, *Look behind the settee.*

It was so big and had
sparkly shiny silver wheels.
I gasped and my mind birled.
I don't know how to ride it.
It's too big.
Someone shouted, *Take it outside.*
My gun belt dropped to the floor.
It's cold, put your jacket on.
The door slammed behind me.
Not a horse but a real bike!

I walked along the road,
pushing it, like real men did.
I never really wanted
to be a cowboy.

Betrayal, 1957
for Lesley

Awkward, shy, but unable to resist,
laughter had drawn her to
the crumbling old pig-sty.
Protesting wire squealed
through rusty staples as
we raced up the shoogly post.
We balanced briefly on barbs,
then scrambled to
thunder-slide on hot,
bum-polished, corrugated iron.
Large, five-year-old eyes,
pled wordlessly to join us.
Friends punched me with smirks
but I shrugged indifference,
and her eyes glowed.
All-too-soon there were whimpers.
"Your sister's stuck," they jeered,
"she can keep off our bit."
She perched, trembling,
staring down, but eventually let go.
Stutter-slipping on untried rust,
she dropped into nettles.
Dusty pain-tracks marked her cheeks
as she stabbed me with red accusing eyes.

Another Cold Morning

The rattle of horizontal rain
and wind's muted moan
penetrates double-glazing,
stirs memories of other days
of dreich northern grey.

I see again vegetables
sprawled on a kitchen table,
a pan simmering,
clouds of steam pumping
into the busy clatter.
She's singing Pet Clark,
warming the dreary day.

Is it dinner time yet?
Her kind smile slips through time,
brushes the moment.
*Take your things off the table
there's a good boy.*
Toy soldiers slip into pockets.
*You can get the cutlery out,
wash your hands first.*

Drips slip on the inside of cold glass,
pooling on the white window-sill.
I swallow hard, drag my hand
across my eyes, open them again.
No condensation here, only warm tears
and rain-drops on the cold outside.

Little Sister
(For Beth)

In winter's dim light, I see your smile
shimmering in the dark window,
drawings scrawled in condensation,
await your poised finger.

The heavy door thuds,
sealing out the cold grey day,
I stoop one-legged and stumble.
My wellie tumbles from numb
fingers, double-clunks on lino,
one woollen sock dangling
from a pale half-naked foot.

Sharp words cut through kitchen steam.
I told you to keep away from the burn.
Get out of those wet things.
A soaking sock schlopps to the floor,
to be whipped up, with a scowl.
Go and get something dry on your feet.

Head hanging, I trudge to the stairs.
You're there, six-years-old,
fingers cold and window-wet,
breathing your quiet concern.
I'll get your slippers if you like,
I know where they are.
So serious! My mood evaporates
and I take my smile upstairs
to search for clean socks.

The Empty Threat

The Raeburn was a magnet on icy
mornings, frozen fingers hovering,
warm above the grey metal plate.
I hope you've taken your boots off.
Blundering into my daydream, her words
rattled in-time with the loose kettle-lid,
. . . and did you get the coal?
I sighed, could almost feel her scowl
reaching down the corridor.
Yes Mum!

On tip-toes, I leant my heat-reddened
face across hot iron to dribble drips
that sizzle-bounced, skittering across
hot steel to die in dusty, rust-red stains.
The slap came from nowhere
but I recognized the ringing dirl.
Dirty, filthy habit!
Scowling, her eyes never left mine,
as she delved into an apron pocket.
Do you want me to tell your father?
Lip salve was applied while she
awaited my response.
Sorry!

Her familiar smile appeared,
beaming through clouds of vapour,
she removed a pan-lid and began to sing.
I started to breathe again.

Learning from You
for Dad

From as far back as I can remember,
you listened with patience to my quick
words, as we laughed and played together.
So many times across the years you'd
draw from me some ill-thought stance
then make some comment,
leave me to absorb and ponder.
You never told me I was wrong
nor laughed at youth's delusions,
you never told me I was right.
You set in motion trains of thought
that helped me grow, fed false argument,
tested me with nonsense, raised my ire.

Reluctance grew to accept your words
or any words unscreened by thought,
I see that now. You forced me to ask
the question, *Why?* taught me to
analyse the motives of others,
to balance actions and outcomes.
I learned to consider all points-of-view,
not to jump to easy judgements, that
the majority are not always right.
I began to distrust the press, to see through
the lies peddled for vested interests and
to question motives, especially my own.
From you I began to glean tolerance,
I learned empathy without knowing it.
You lent me life's map. You sowed the seeds.

The Salmon Rod
for Dad

Split cane, four crafted sections,
lacquered, resting in my tired hands,
drawing memories that rise like salmon
surging through the years.

Too weighty for a child to bear
and yet so light within your practiced grip.
The Spey was for you alone,
but on the Beatshach Burn,
above the burbling ford, *we* fished.
I see the peat-stained waters rush
and tumble round mossy stones.
Your silent silhouette poised
in wind-rushed-air's embrace,
the practiced flick of wrist
beside the restless rowan.
I hear the swish that sends the tip,
and see the snaking lash,
the flash of line, the fall and plop
into the dark, still pool
where brown trout lurk.

No need for words, eyes say it all
when bound so close in silence.
Lifting your head you send that smile
. . . and cast again.

Under Naked Trees

As colour drains from trees,
unnoticed shadows grow and gather,
indistinct, enigmatic, lurking in
gloom and stealthy silence.

Night creeps, spreads through low
bare boughs, in deepening dingy-grey,
whilst lost in thought, I shuffle on,
distracted and alone.

My mind grasps at impatient stars,
probes where abstract daydreams surge,
to soar above this forest grim,
these fading lonely leaves.

As light departs, intrigue convenes,
gathering in the frosty dark,
inciting my romantic dreams
at withering day's demise.

Gracenotes

A stark silhouette
stamped on sky's deep blue.
Eyes absorb stars,
emerging, fading, pulsing
beyond knowledge,
tiny white seeds spinning,
scattered on indigo
floating in the void.

Hair-shadows flutter
in night's cool breath,
slipping misty whispers
of white noise thrumming
through the universe.
Tingling chord-sequences
shiver on neck-hairs,
seeding a silent smile.

Solitude

Pale and frail, your ghost lingers in my space,
its presence fills my reflective world.
Itinerant clues are willowy, wandering,
hard to gather, to assemble into meaning.
Solitary tears slip through my silence.

Sometimes, a memory of your soft scent wafts
through fuzzy thoughts, fumbles at the stiff door
of acceptance. Words are sluggish, form strings in
mumbled pieces, while my unfocussed eyes
view only vague and shapeless things.

Forsaken, lost and lonely, I grope for answers,
finding none. With shrugs and sighs, I probe the
empty silences where once your laughter sang.
I have no plans for what's to come, just drift
and wander endless hours alone, with you.

Now You're Gone

Absorbed in dreams, oblivious to the world,
we took no time to think ahead, drifting
through long carefree days, our smiles
flickering through summer showers.

Here yellow grasses cling,
broken-stemmed and lifeless beside
the forest path we used to know.
Beneath an uncertain sun, Autumn's
branches reach for empty skies,
wet silence dripping on the boles of oaks.
Grey clouds gather, a pigeon's plaintive
call echoes through naked trees, cold
winds sighing on rough and fissured skin.

My pale fingers trace your photo's face,
now kissed only by misty breath.
Memories linger in this empty place.
Tear-drops trickle as it starts to rain
again.

Divining Destiny

Anticipation sleeps in cold woods,
a dark wind is rising, gathering
momentum, groaning through
the limbs of yesterday's trees.
An unknown future looms.

I listen for clues, the plastic clock
on my wall ticking-off doubts,
the firm click of a closing door
ends it all, shuts out the past.
There is no whisper of loss,
no nostalgia for what's forgotten.

A worn rose-tinted diary loaded
with pen-scratched aspirations,
lies closed on an unlit desk,
witness and record of regret.
A new one lies beside it, fresh
white pages full of promise.

The Spell of 'Story'

Bathed in stillness, eyes focussed,
the world has disappeared.
In the peaceful quiet,
a lone bright light sets each page on fire.
Evening draws her grey skirts close,
sinuous chill encroaches,
sliding through cool silence.

Cold from immobility, I shiver.
Tiny sounds impinge, tremble
through weakening concentration.
Clicks and ticks and creaks that
smother workings of the mind,
destroy that magic link.

Rising, I stretch and yawn,
await the turgid tide,
mundane reality trundling into focus.
Though story fades and drifts away,
the dreams endure, ideas tasted that
taunt and tease, until the next time.

Waking in the Night at Moniack Mhòr

Writers' dreams are woven
through this building's fabric,
percolating in pipes,
seeping through soft darkness.
Contracting timbers creak,
the patient walls whispering
inspiration as they cool and settle,
dispersing shared ideas and visions
leached from wandering thought.
But enlightenment is grey,
haunted by false dawns
and spiders.

Sharing Words

You comment on capricious words
that stumble from my hand.
The dreams are mine, I only share them,
let you breathe them for a while.

They come to me with purpose,
form themselves inside my mind,
then linger on the edges taunting me to
write them down before they disappear.
They never come the same way twice
and, if I fail to claim them for my tale
they tease, with glimpses
of what might have been.
When fixed upon a paper's skin
I find that more words tumble forth
to play and slide upon the waiting page,
then more, and sometimes even more.

Often words mislead me,
leave me blind to what comes next.
I make no claim of right nor wrong,
of good nor bad, their story simply is.

Turning Leaves

On the opening of Nairn's new bookshop,
Saturday 21ˢᵗ November, 2015.

Nairn's grey pavements frost-glisten
on this bleak November day.
Funnelled icy air blasts from dim alleys.
Dry leaves scrape and tumble,
their dull song rattling
down an empty High Street.
The bookshop door closes,
excluding dreariness with a click.

Bathed in brightness,
beneath sparkly chandeliers,
bulging shelves draw wandering
eyes to teasing, tempting treasures.
Mavis circulates like warm air,
fuelling fervent chatter.
In this new haven of books,
excitement simmers, flickers,
flares on faces as
the leaves keep turning.

Monday Morning

On Monday Mornings,
beneath an olive tree, etched on glass,
friends meet in the tranquillity
that wordsmiths crave.

Relaxation amidst chatter,
cutlery clatters with crockery.
Soon plates bear only lonely crumbs,
cups are empty and gossip dwindles.
Anticipation grows, papers emerge
from bags, are passed around.

Opinions sharpen, huddled heads nod.
Slipping from paper,
teasing text-sequences play on lips.
Words are weighed and tossed,
retained or lost,
and sometimes re-arranged.

An ambience of warmth
pervades the *Olive Tree Café*,
a creative essence, nourishing, secure.

Memory Drifting
for Shonagh

Dry litter crunches underfoot.
Memories wake, meander through this dim,
still, place, beneath aged, brooding oaks.
Mind-wandering in flickering light,
the brief rumour of our passing barely
scratches time in this hoary wood.

On the forest track, lush, green and
flower-speckled, small, pale, butterflies skip.
I see my sister breeze-dancing in a light
summer frock, flouncing in sunlight,
fluttering with birch-leaves.
The vision dissolves in scolding wren's
displeasure as she flits unseen through
tangles of woodbine and shade.

Daze-drifting round corners, I stop.
Hungry insects whirl and drone,
uncertainty loiters in the pulsing air.
A roe-deer stands motionless, frozen.
Dark, fearful eyes are locked on mine,
rousing memories of a little girl
poised high on a garage roof,
tight curls white on air-bronzed skin,
anxious blue eyes wide and wary.
The moment passes.
Alone again, on the woodland path,
the warm breeze whispers down the years,
Sorry Dad!

Father of the Bride

Unruly tears trickle down my smile.
Your confident, flushed elation,
radiates joy and fills my world.
As you turn in the light,
that familiar child-like grin
illuminates your rascal face.
Pleasure-sparkles swim in your eyes.
Smiling guests whisper approval
as I try to catch your gaze,
try to send you my love.
Prickly tingles tease my neck-hairs,
I seek composure-time, alone;
but I'm mirror-ambushed
by a ridiculously, silly smirk.

Picnic Table Reminiscence
For Mum

Breeze ruffled daydreams drift
in a green glass jug.
Impatient ice-cubes rattle,
condensation slips onto silvered wood.

Through translucent shadows
memory of your smile
spills over dark wet rings,
tumbles into sighs.

The wind rises through whispers,
willow's fronds lurch skywards,
a blue plastic cup leaps off the table,
startling sparrows into histrionic panic.

Blue tits, chittering delight, range back
and forth playing chasing games
in their best bright jumpers,
nobody tells them to put on old clothes.

You seemed ageless to busy youth,
with your quiet smiling patience.
As you loiter on daydream's fringes,
I take tea with your ghost.

On the Dunes at Covesea

Here, at the ocean's margin,
the short dry grass is strewn
with thrift and violets.
I lie, slumped in a sandy hollow,
high in dunes of whipping marram,
bathing in the salt-sea's scent.
On the beach below, foraging
sandpipers peep excitement,
their forward-rush synchronized
to each retreating wave.

In hot sun's glare, red shades
of bobbing grasses flicker
through closed eyelids
rousing childhood ghosts.
Screaming gulls wheel above and
I'm aware of my mother, once more
squatting beside me, dib-dabbing
with calamine lotion.
Hold still, she chides, as she laughs
at my lack of patience.

Time passes, clouds obscure
the light and brightness fades.
Rising as the sun heads west,
she stretches tired, stiff legs,
and gradually fades, her smile
dissolving into grey evening.
My old knees ache as I rise too,
mirroring her movement,
shared stiffness transcending time.

Nursing my Empty Cup

Looking backwards
I see empty roads,
lines of wires bowing
in the ceaseless wind.

Children's laughter lingers
behind the ruined steading
where we used to play,
swirling round crumbling eaves,
in sunlight, with swallows,
disappearing into the blue
distances of morning.

I see you skipping
through yellow autumn,
light-flickers kissing
your sun-bleached hair;
pulling dry grasses,
fingers filled with seeds.

But then grey-Winter
evenings come again,
and I wonder, like yesterday
and the day before.

The black and white cat
stalks past my window,
he's searching too,
but he won't find out.

*I've been here longer
than any of you,
and still don't know.*

Journey to the Post-box

The world dissolves.
I lumber forward,
distracted by simmering rage.
Bouncing sparrows
frolic in my path.
Yellow mats of pine-pollen
drift on breeze-rippled puddles.
A sudden ice-cold shock jolts
from foot to brain and the
road-slap of my wet slipper
starts a ginger cat across my path.
At lane's end,
excited bird-song
re-ignites the day.
Hungry hedge-fingers
clutch at warm sunlight
as I post my letter of complaint.
On the bones of a naked elm
a crow cocks her head
and seems to know.

The Old Settee

Plump lips slip and play,
tongues tease wine-glass rims.
Giggling, bending to sit,
gentle brushing fingers sweep
the surface of wrinkled hide.
Sleek young thighs
glide onto waiting upholstery,
sensuous sighs greeting
its soft lingering caress.
To the muted squeak
of flesh on leather,
warm round buttocks sink
into cushioned depths.

How many close encounters
can I bear, at my age?

Park Bench

Here dreams are dusted-down, plans made,
lives weighed, and balanced, fates sealed.
Torn inside, desperate for enlightenment,
the troubled wallow in emotional turbulence,
pursue unlikely possibilities, seek evasive answers,
while they shake their heads and weep.

Benign beneath swaying boughs of beech,
stroked by soft sunlight and gentle air,
the wooden bench awaits the next encounter.
Flaking paint denying its true importance;
it sits as it has always done, tired and worn,
awaiting a new sensory tsunami.

The 'Old Boys' Group Photograph

His long white hair and beard
flutter in cool air's caress,
banners of honour and service.

Almost isolated amidst the many,
jacket hanging open, convention ignored,
he twirls his hardwood stick.
Time-stamped in sepia, his eyes
search beyond the camera,
brief-thought re-treading the catalogue
of years, lingering over absent friends.

Senses sift through fading summers,
the whispering song of a swinging scythe,
the sweet scent of new-mown grass.
Faint wisps of tobacco-smoke waft,
twisting through sunlight, tangling
with ghostly breaths of childhood-laughter,
the rhythmic creak of a rope swing.

His dark eyes focus on distance,
delve in drifts of memory, visit again
those moments which mattered most.

Nairn Harbour

Weather-worn, in winter's bright crisp light,
the old man stands alone, sailing on memory.

There are no piles of nets waiting to be loaded,
no green-glass buoys, no empty creels, no tarry
wooden boxes piled on a crowded bustling quay.
Like yesterdays, they've slipped away.
Once the daring walked these walls,
braved the frigid firth for fish and gambled
their lives on the North Sea's whim.
The harbour reverberated to yelling voices,
clattering fish-boxes, the squeal of pulleys,
and the slap and flap of heavy canvas.
Keening gulls circled in the cold grey sky,
bathing in the ever-present stink of fish.

No squat cottages remain, end-on to the gale,
no small dark windows ever watching.
Now graceless modern buildings stand,
uncomfortable in this place, their tiled lichen-
covered roofs replace the hard clean glint of slate.
Mirror-water silver-shimmers in quiet silence,
line-reflections of yacht masts dance,
their ripples synchronised to the rhythm
of dangling ropes wind-rattling on aluminium.
Only lonely pleasure-craft bob
and wallow in this lifeless basin.

Bearing a basket, a bronze fisherwoman,
unperturbed and settled in this place,
stands frozen in time's grey moment.

The Tolbooth, Forres

Puddled reflections, flashes of green,
red and amber pierce black-velvet,
wash the night with gaudy brightness.
Funnelling through wynds and closes,
wind-songs whisper of days gone by.
No horses clop on cobble stones,
no hawkers haunt this High Street.
Only name-shadows evoke the toun's past,
Hangman's Well, Castle Hill, Bogton.

Enduring, the Tolbooth stands
rooted in this place, a symbol
of continuity and permanence.
The stocky building towers, dark,
staunch, immovable in driving rain.
Bastion against time's slow passage,
brooding in the town's living heart,
remembering the glory-days.
Ill-used through the gloom of years,
claimed at last by those who care.

The Lizard Lord of Delos

Blue and speckled, he languishes
on an edge of broken masonary
in this ancient temple of Apollo.
Tongue flicking, catching insects
in a warm updraft, he watches me
breathe deep in oppressive heat.

His smaller cousins skate the ground,
he's in a good spot, a survivor.
Tiredness dilutes energy to dry dust,
I raise my hand to wipe . . .
and he's gone,
like the peoples of the past.

I remember other lonely ruins,
dreich hills call to me
across the foreign distance,
with promises of cold, clean air,
and soft, rain-soaked skies,
of walks that soak my jeans
leaving my legs speckled in
grass-seed confetti.

Cool drops ghosting down my neck
turn into hot, wet, sweat.
The relentless sun drains resolve
pummels my listless will.
I wipe my brow as I squint
through hot blue haze.
Dust catches in my throat
but as I begin to wish . . .
I remember midgies.

Momentary Presence

Beyond the ship's rail, floating on dreams,
the surface of the Aegean flickers and glistens.
The blue Cyclades, drift on the near horizon,
their roots hidden in mist, haze-shrouded in myth.
Scatters of white houses speckle the tired shore-line,
glinting in harsh sunlight, defying the draining heat,
their frail existence enduring time's harsh toll.

Almost beyond knowledge, on the edge of the world,
the Hebrides rise, sharp and clear in memory,
black, cold and determined, they fight for survival,
their roots hidden in mist, haze-shrouded in myth.
Scatters of white houses cling to a rugged shore-line,
scoured by Atlantic gales, defying the driving rain,
their frail existence enduring time's harsh toll.

As the foam of passage dissolves
behind us, transient worlds drift
between past and present,
their momentary presence erased
by time's relentless surge.

Devastation

Evidence abounds: no oaks remain,
no pines to deny crimes perpetrated,
only memories of trees linger in thin soil.
Stunted rowan, pockets of gale-ripped
birch endure, torn by relentless change.
Gnarled toes delve in lichen encrusted
scree, clinging to their place in this world,
survivors from the times of burning,
and the ravenous teeth of sheep.
Overgrown with years, deserted runs and rigs,
abandoned peat banks and lonely tumbled
ruins, all cry out to eyes that read the land.

The people are gone with their ragged cattle,
their joy and colour, cleared like the forests.
All that remains is a playground for
deer stalkers and grouse-shooters.
Relentless air sweeps over grass and heather,
the grim years slide, the heart torn from a land
numbed, stunned, weeping in transient winds,
still digesting its disbelief.
Perplexed spirits watch visitors arrive in fine
coaches to view this desert, to marvel at empty
glens and the laird's fine house, hear them absorb
the lies of incomers, the descendants of imported
shepherds and gamekeepers.

But the land endures, it's story told
and re-told in in the skylark's song,
the laughter of running water
and the whispers of lonely air.

Veiled in Shadow

Wretched rubble lies in piles
around crumbling unroofed walls.
Inside, a foxglove, tall and strong,
shelters from the wild west wind,
Luss na ban sidhe she is called,
the flower of the fairy-woman.
Here, time's rippling shadow
ponders shards of shattered slate
and rotting, worm-riddled rafters.

Nearby, a silvered wooden gate
sags in a tumble of grey dyke.
Stubborn thistles toss amongst
trembling grasses, straining to
resist buffeting blast and bluster.
Half-buried in nettles, a coil
of rusting fence-wire leeches
oxides into thin and stony ground.

No peat-smoke stains the icy air.
The glen is empty of cattle and song.
Joyless and forgotten fields, choked,
smothered with encroaching bracken,
crave the warmth of sun on soil.
Only the wind sighs, remembering
the laughter of yesterday's children.

The Lion's Growing Restless

" ... is Alba lobhadh an suain bhreoite" – Somhairle Macgill-ean
" ... *and Scotland mouldering in sick slumber*" – *Sorley MacLean*

The ignorant and unwary walk among us
in the manner of sheep sharing grazing,
unaware of restlessness and agitatation.
They absorb the oft-repeated lies without
question, without thought, oblivious to
strengthening currents, the undertow
that may soon sweep them away.

Our people are disenfranchised,
dispossessed by an alien establishment,
an uncaring government that
bends the rules, looks after its own.

The wind is changing, a storm is coming.
Troubled eyes glance at the sky.
People shake their heads.
Unsettling currents sweep through
the collective consciousness, carrying
and lifting folk, forcing them to think.
Authority's false direction is viewed anew,
the condescending words that don't
ring true, the great lie of democracy,
the corporate greed, the arrogance.

An agitated people are awakening at last,
searching for a new direction.

Glenfiddich

Only sheep linger in this silent glen.
The breathing of the vanished
rustles through autumn rowans,
the past engulfing me,
soaking into hummocks,
weeping in the wind.
Locked in layers of time,
the 'other world' still lingers,
peaty waters rumbling in the
shallows of yesterday's ford,
shades of long-haired cattle
bellowing in birch-shadow.

A ghost beneath the metal bridge,
the drover stares back at me,
darkness tumbling from his gaze.
Pained memories leech
from cairns of tumbled stones
where homes once stood.
In barren fields of short whipped grass
shadows flicker of long-dead trees,
forests where old pathways wander,
twisting through restless wind-songs.

The Edge of Reason

Fragile wind-breaths roam
this murmuring land of shade,
slipping under low branches,
stirring frail, pale foliage.
Stark, striped shadows oscillate
through birdsong and agitated boughs.
Strange eddies stir in heavy air,
stick-fingers snap in unseen corners,
restless leaves whisper in thickets,
rustling, drifting, numbing thought.

My vacant eyes drift, gaze
through imagination's window,
day-dreams probe beyond
understanding, tease just out of reach.
Neck hairs scream silent messages,
darkening my light as comprehension
flounders on this restless afternoon.
Secrets beyond logic
stalk the edge of reason.

The Gift of Knowledge

Plunk. A stone sinks to stillness
in the depths of a dingy pool.
Snaggled in shade the salmon hovers,
poised among dangling roots.
Splash. Silver surface-circles widen,
a cone bobs on light-ripples.
Unblinking eyes find a child
shadow-flitting on the river-bank
amidst fluttering hazels.

River roars his restless song,
churning waters edged with dirty foam,
tumble over jagged rocks.
Waiting, hidden beneath pummelling
froth and bubbles, Fate clutches the
pale-skinned boy, drags him to oblivion.
Water-choked and strangely calm,
he floats and drifts in dreams.
Then, face to face with salmon's lidless
eyes, a numb contentment grows inside.
Knowledge flows in streams of long
pale light, then all goes dark.

Restless alders shiver in careless air.
Bright beams of sunlight halo clouds
and the warm wind gutters.
Cruising crows witness a momentous event.
Spluttering, face-down on shingle,
coughs fight through gulps and gasps.
A head rises, lank hair drips,
young eyes register shock, then,
a slow smile gathers . . . and he knows.

The Goddess of Winter

Thick flakes tumble from growing gloom,
movement fills the expectant night,
snow flurries thicken, merge into endless blur.
Beara is burying the world beneath her new
white plaid, stifling the past, as the old year dies.
There is no solidity in this relentless movement,
grey-white shadows shifting at vision's edge,
air impregnated with stealthy silence.

Fell-voices whisper between looming tree-shadows,
steady snow-fall on this the old-year's longest night.
Pitiless, endless, settling through darkness,
dying, sinking into the obscurity of memory.
Chill breath-clouds scrape my cheeks, dissolving,
vanishing, to join the past in eternal cold.

The Yule log, carved for the crone, is put to the fire,
pale faces, gather to watch it burn,
dreams focused, anxious for this dark year's end.
Hopes surge as flames consume the ancient birch,
frozen memories joining the dead.
Outside, on this the first day of a bright new year,
wooden limbs reach upwards, stretching
for returning light and new beginnings.

Watching

Flapping, frantic, from the red-barked pine
they rise, a restless, ragged, cloud of black,
agitated, cawing, circling to the west,
their raucous racket dying with distance.

Bathed in flecks of sunlight and water-gurgle,
immersed in meditation, Old Willow broods.
As dark waters pass the ancient ford,
he monitors leaf-rustle and bee-messages,
his knobbly fingers scratch the silent surface,
sifting possibilities. Light-sparkles drift
downstream, cruise the careless current,
bathe in sunlight's flickering promise.
Willow sees the heaving horde depart,
three crows remain, the 'Three as One,'
he knows the skin they wear.

Growing air-blasts slap the canopy,
crash like seas of surging waves on shingle.
Hints of mocking laughter taint a rising wind,
tug at leaf-tremble, rush through roiling foliage.
Willow's long strands flail and roar in rapture
as branches crack and wooden fingers snap.
High boughs bouncing, tossing twigs,
send sticks and leaves a-tumbling.

But all-too-soon excitement fades and trees
regain their breath. As Willow settles down
to brood again, oblivious to whisperings and
wind-change, three crows patrol warm air.
Ominous, ever alert, they are watching too.

Restless

I hadn't really noticed the crows before,
gathering on roof-tops, waiting in trees,
distracting, prodding me with their presence.

Your voice ambushes me in quiet moments.
I hear your faint whispers in leaf-rustle, in
the swish of grasses, in the wind's soft sigh.
Fleeting movements tease in eye-corners,
glint from the shoulders of wine bottles
glimmer on passing windscreens.
Sometimes I see your face reflected in the
mirrored depths of my red and empty eyes.

Crows trail after me to the hills,
raggedly flapping through cool air's rush.
I hear your voice in the music of tumbling water,
your warm laughter, as summer raindrops
play on the skin of a mountain-pool,
your smile dissolving as ripples
slide across its slick darkness.

As I stand alone before the restless ocean,
Crow watches from the edge of dunes,
her dark rags fluttering in my heartache.
Your scent drifts on salt-sea bluster,
echoes teasing through rushing air.
Are you with me still, shadow-watching
while I struggle with impossibility?

My mind drifts onto paths
where none should wander,
casting for answers that can't be found.

Walking in Darkness

False confidence is dangerous, unwise,
a hidden truth that skirts discomfort's edge,
as sun goes down unbidden fears arise.

Unease unfolds to scorn and criticize
the darkest phantoms that a mind can dredge.
False confidence is dangerous, unwise.

The whispering wind sings songs of grim surprise,
black-rumours bubble, rising up through sedge.
As sun goes down unbidden fears arise.

Nerves multiply at certainty's demise,
illusion, pre-conception, you allege.
False confidence is dangerous, unwise.

Mischievous changes, hard to recognize,
shadow-shrouds that drift through leaf and hedge.
As sun goes down unbidden fears arise.

Capricious concepts clad in strange disguise,
neck-prickles tease as nightmares grow and fledge.
False confidence is dangerous, unwise.
As sun goes down unbidden fears arise.

In My Chair

Evening light is thin and grey,
my mind still spinning the wheel
of that upturned wooden barrow,
unsure of the question, trying
to find an answer that might fit.
As tired moments tick towards tomorrow
I sigh, sore eyes closing to welcome
the warmth of uncertain darkness.

Mountain air agitates seas of heather,
bites my neck, a touch that stirs my soul,
it is a part of me, like peat-smoke.
Crags, trees and dark-skies loom,
rushing water tumbles, somewhere.
Always there is the slide of wind,
moving, whispering, screaming,
crying, as an eagle scratches slow
dark circles high in clear, cold blue.

Then you're here beside me,
a teasing grin, patient eyes a-sparkle
with that gleam of knowing.
You turn the barrow upside-down as you
always do and I know I'll see you soon.
Wakening to pained yowls, I find the dog
twitching, chasing rabbits in his dream.
A small orange glow flickers in a dying fire.
Someone's put the light out.

NOTES

Page 14   **Sleepers:** Some old railway sleepers, erected on-end as a snow-fence to shelter exposed sections of the line from drifting snow. Some still remain in place.

Page 22   **High Above the Black Loch's Skin:** The name of the mountain 'Chuinneag,' (spelt 'Quinag,' in English) means a milking pail in Gaelic.

Page 31   **Seaforth Villa, Carron, 1954:** The Puggie was a small locomotive used to pull the local Speyside train in the 1950's.

Page 45   **Waking in the Night at Moniack Mhòr:** Moniack Mhòr is the name of the writer's centre high in the hills near Abriachan, above Loch Ness.

Page 58   **Nairn Harbour:** A bronze statue of a fisherwoman with a creel stands beside Nairn Harbour.

Page 67   **The Gift of Knowledge:** In Celtic myth the salmon is viewed as the bearer of all knowledge.

Page 68   **The Goddess of Winter:** As mid-winter and the solstice approached, Beara, the goddess of winter, would wash the evils of the old year from her plaid in the whirlpool, Coire Bhreacain until it was white, pure and free of blemish. She laid her new white plaid across the land (snowfall) to clean it of evil, to provide for a new beginning. A Highland variation of the Yule-log tradition saw the head of the household carve a birch stump into the likeness of an old woman. At dusk, the carved figure was brought into the house, lain upon the burning peat of the house fire. Burning her, was thought to drive away the winter and protect the occupants of the household from death. The family would gather round to watch the figure consumed. The carved figure on the yule-log, represents evils of the year gone, winter and death. It had to be totally consumed by the fire if misfortune and death were to be averted in the coming year. Strangers who arrived with an extra piece of fuel increased the chances of completely destroying the 'yule log,' hence the welcome for a first-foot with an extra piece of fuel.

Indigo Dreams Publishing Ltd
24, Forest Houses
Cookworthy Moor
Halwill
Beaworthy
Devon
EX21 5UU
www.indigodreams.co.uk